What Did the Princess Find?

and other Questions

By Sally Ann Wright • Illustrated by Paola Bertolini Grudina

What did Abraham want?

A baby son!

God had promised him a huge family,
as many children as stars in the sky.
But it was many years before
his wife Sarah had baby Isaac.
Then God blessed them
with grandchildren
and great grandchildren,
and great great grandchildren –
a very big family.

What did Esau eat?

A bowl of lentil soup!

Esau had been out all day and was so hungry,
he told his brother he would give anything
to eat what he was cooking.
So Jacob gave him the soup.
But in return Esau gave him the special blessing
that a father should only give to his first son.

What did Joseph wear?

A beautiful coloured coat!

It made his brothers so jealous that
they made sure he was sent away
to a strange land to live.
But God had plans for Joseph.
God kept Joseph safe in Egypt
so he could help his family many years later.

What did the princess find?

A baby in a basket!

Moses was hidden there
to keep him safe
from the soldiers.

The princess wanted to keep him.
So she let him grow up in the palace.
When Moses was grown up
God helped him to save his people.

What did Solomon build?

A beautiful temple!

Solomon loved God so much that
he wanted to build a beautiful building
so people could come to worship him.
Solomon chose the finest wood
and the best silver and gold
to make a very special gift for God.

What did the shepherds see?

Bright shining angels!

The shepherds were looking after their sheep
when the angels came to tell them
that baby Jesus had been born in Bethlehem.
They ran to see the special baby
who would bring peace to the world,
and found him lying in a manger.

What did the fishermen catch?

Lots of fish!

Peter and Andrew had caught nothing all night
but Jesus told them to let down their nets
in the deeper water of Lake Galilee.

The nets became so full of fish that
James and John had to come and help them!
Then Jesus asked the fishermen to be his disciples.

What did the soldier need?

A word from Jesus!

The Roman soldier had a servant who was very ill.
He didn't want to bother Jesus.
He didn't even need him to come to his house!

'I know you can help him,' he said.
'Just say the word and I know he'll be well.'
So Jesus did – and the soldier's servant got better.

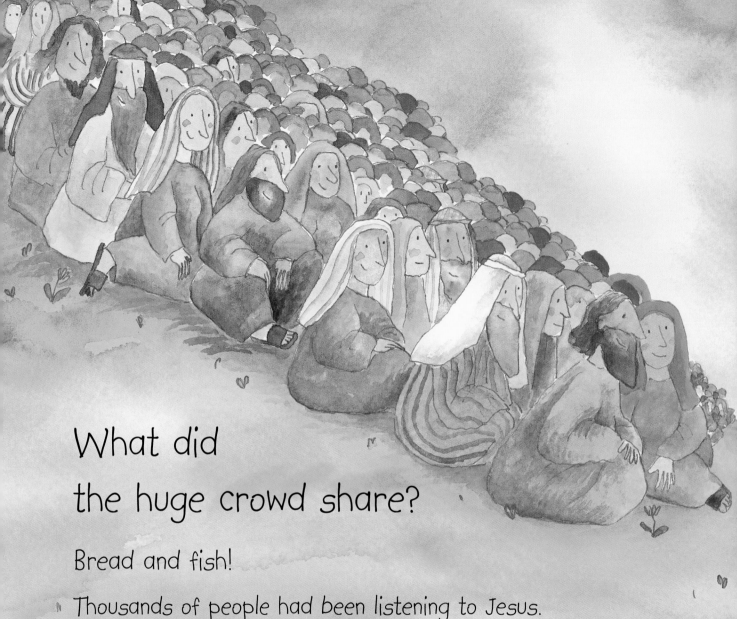

What did
the huge crowd share?

Bread and fish!

Thousands of people had been listening to Jesus.
Jesus saw that they were hungry and he wanted to help.
Andrew found a boy with five rolls and two little fish.

The boy gave his lunch to Jesus,
and Jesus thanked God and shared it out...
and everyone had enough to eat and some left over!

What did the kind man do?

He looked after his neighbour.

Jesus told a story about a dying man.
First a priest had walked past without helping.
Then another religious man did the same.
It was a man from another country who stopped,
bathed the man's wounds and put him on his own donkey.
Jesus said this man had pleased God.

What did the leper say?

Thank you!

Jesus met ten men
who had a skin disease.
They couldn't live normal lives.
No one would come near them.
So when they asked him,
Jesus made them well.
Nine men went away,
happy to be healed.
Only one came back to thank Jesus.

What did the widow give?

Everything she had!

The rich men gave lots of money
to the temple.
But they still had plenty left over.
Jesus told his disciples that
the widow had given more
than any of them.
Her two copper coins
were all she had,
but she had given them to God.

What did Jesus ride?

A donkey!

Two of the disciples put cloaks over the donkey's back.
Jesus sat on it and rode into Jerusalem.
Crowds of people were going there for the festival.
They spread their cloaks on the ground.
They waved palm branches in the air.
'Hooray for Jesus the King!'
they shouted.

Published in the UK by Bible Reading Fellowship
First Floor, Elsfield Hall, Oxford OX2 8FG England
ISBN 1 84101 438 9

First edition 2006

Editorial Director Annette Reynolds
Art Director Gerald Rogers
Pre-production Krystyna Hewitt
Production John Laister

Stories can be found in the Bible as follows:
What did Abraham want? Genesis 12:1-2; 21:1-8
What did Esau eat? Genesis 25:27-33
What did Joseph wear? Genesis 37, 46
What did the princess find? Exodus 2:1-10
What did Solomon build? 1 Kings 6:1-38
What did the shepherds see? Luke 2:8-16
What did the fishermen catch? Luke 5:1-11
What did the soldier need? Matthew 8:5-13
What did the huge crowd share? John 6:1-13
What did the kind man do? Luke 10:30-37
What did the leper say? Luke 17:11-19
What did the widow give? Luke 21:1-4
What did Jesus ride? Mark 11:1-10

Printed and bound in Singapore